THE LAST DAYS
≈ OF ≈
WESTERN
STEAM

**FROM THE BILL REED
COLLECTION**

THE LAST DAYS

OF

WESTERN STEAM

FROM THE BILL REED COLLECTION

In Full Colour

PETER TUFFREY

FONTHILL

Above: Aberystwyth Station 7803
At rest on Aberystwyth station's platform three during July 1962 was G.W.R. 'Manor' Class locomotive no. 7803 *Barcote Manor*. The engine would subsequently leave with the 10.10 a.m. service to Shrewsbury.

Previous Page: Worcester Shed 5096
Collett 'Castle' Class 4-6-0 no. 5096 *Bridgwater Castle* was a visitor at Worcester shed on 7th April 1962. Construction of the engine had occurred at Swindon Works in June 1936 and no. 5096 was the penultimate member of the class to enter traffic before the Second World War. The number of 'Castles' would increase after the cessation of the conflict.

Fonthill Media Limited
Fonthill Media LLC
www.fonthillmedia.com
office@fonthillmedia.com

First published 2014

ISBN 978-1-78155-301-5

Printed in England

Contents

Carmarthen Station 4962

'Hall' Class engine no. 4962 *Ragley Hall* departs from Carmarthen station with a service bound for the north on 21st April 1962. The station was opened on 1st July 1902 by the G.W.R. and replaced facilities placed on a site just to the north. The company responsible for this latter railway stop was the Carmarthen & Cardigan Railway and Carmarthen Town, as it was later known, operated from the beginning of March 1860. No. 4962 would be in service for a further three years after this image was captured, being condemned at Oxford during October 1965.

Acknowledgements

I would like to thank the following people for their help: Iris Chambers; Peter Jary; Hugh Parkin; Bill Reed.

Gratitude should also be expressed to my son Tristram for his help behind the scenes.

Introduction

Despite recently turning 81 years of age, life-long Nottingham resident Bill Reed has still got an insatiable appetite for photographing steam locomotives. A recent stay in York to capture the comings and goings of the summer railtour season testifies to this as when a ban was placed on steam operations in area, Bill travelled to Scotland and Carlisle in order to satisfy his 'need for steam.'

Bill can trace this love of steam (he also enjoys photographing traction engines) to his early childhood as a local journey to visit his aunt would be taken by Sentinel Steam Railcar. Two of the regulars operating the service were no. 5192 Rising Sun and no. 51908 Expedition. By the age of ten, Bill had acquired his first *ABC of British Locomotives* by Ian Allan. This allowed him to recognise the many types in operation on the ex-Great Central line which ran at the bottom of his father's allotment, and where Bill spent many hours doing little work during his formative years.

Upon leaving school, Bill decided that he wanted to pursue a career on the railways. The only vacancy he could find was as a messenger lad at Nottingham Victoria station and it was here that, one day during his lunch break, Bill encountered local photographer Freddie Guildford. He encouraged the young man to take pictures of locomotives and offered to impart his knowledge of developing film. Bill's camera around this time was a Kodak 127 with perforated bellows.

In early 1950, Bill finally obtained a job with locomotives, albeit as a cleaner, joining the staff of Nottingham depot and starting on the road to becoming a driver, which was his ambition. Bill's joy at starting his new career was short lived, however, as National Service recruited him and the next few years were spent with the Royal Corps of Signals in Singapore. One of the duties undertaken by Bill was being a guard at the military hospital and this was one of the more enjoyable times, he says, as the post allowed him to watch the trains passing on the line to Kuala Lumpur.

British Railways provided Bill a position as a fireman, again at Nottingham, when demobbed in 1955 and at this time he purchased an Agfa Super Isolette camera. This was used to take pictures, not only of the motive power in the Nottingham area, but locomotives in operation around the country. Bill travelled extensively during the late 1950s and early 1960s capturing the new and the old engines at work in the respective regions of B.R. During this time Bill acquired a Canon 35 mm colour camera and also used a Bolex 8 mm cine camera.

This collection of over 150 colour photographs, which date from 1958 to 1967, features the Western Region of B.R., formerly the territory of the Great Western Railway, and its motive power. Bill took the pictures during a number of visits to stations, sheds and to areas offering an attractive vantage point to shoot film. He has managed to capture a wide selection of the region's locomotives and these include; 'King' Class, 'Hall' Class, 'Grange' Class and 'County' Class 4-6-0s; Churchward '4300' Class 2-6-0s and '2800' 2-8-0s; Collett 2-6-2T, 0-4-2T and 0-6-0PT designs. A few examples of Swindon's diesel-hydraulic locomotives are also present as well as gas turbine locomotive no. 18000 and an eight-car 'Blue Pullman' set.

The engines have been pictured at various locations around the Western Region, ranging from; Barmouth and Aberystwyth in north west Wales to Whitland in the south west; Crewe and Wellington in the north east to London Paddington, Oxford and Princes Risborough in the south east. The places one would generally associate with the Western Region are also present and they comprise; Swindon (depot, station and works), Bristol, Exeter, Newton Abbot, Truro and Penzance.

Bill has taken photographs of locomotives working on a number of branch lines around the Western Region and these are particularly evocative of the era. They also point to the future, in the form of the Beeching Report, when mass closures occurred eliminating these stations serving the local communities. The branch line stations featured are often deserted and the carriages partially empty. In some instances the stations would never serve many people, but others would lose passengers after the rise in motor car use in the wake of the Second World War. The W.R. attempted to entice passengers to some lines with diesel railcars, also reducing costs, and an example is seen in this collection at Kemble station. The G.W.R. had also tried this tactic with their own railcars and two have been captured at Worcester.

While some readers may note the omission of certain places or engine types they feel are important to the W.R., the intention of the author has been to provide a broad view of the area and the locomotives at work in the last years before the diesel takeover. Thankfully, Bill's enthusiasm for steam has made this fascinating collection possible.

Bill Reed poses for the camera at Looe station during mid-1956 with Churchward '4500' Class 2-6-2T locomotive no. 4552.

The Last Days of Western Steam

Aberystwyth Station 7818
Great Western Railway 'Manor' Class 4-6-0 locomotive no. 7818 *Granville Manor* is standing at the head of the 9.10 a.m. service from Aberystwyth station to Carmarthen on 7th July 1962. The engine was constructed at Swindon Works during January 1939 to the design of Charles Collett and was in traffic for 26 years, being withdrawn in the same month of 1965. No. 7818 was allocated to Machynlleth shed at this time and had been based there from January 1960.

Above

Aberystwyth Station 7800

Another 'Manor' Class engine in attendance at Aberystwyth on 7th July 1962 was no. 7800 *Torquay Manor*, which is at the head of the 12.45 p.m. express passenger service from the station to Crewe. The locomotive resided at Oswestry shed at the time of this photograph and had been allocated there since September 1958. A move would soon follow, however, taking Torquay Manor to Shrewsbury in February 1963 and the locomotive would spend its final year at the depot as withdrawal occurred in August 1964.

Opposite

Aberystwyth Station 7803

G.W.R. 'Manor' Class 4-6-0 no. 7803 *Barcote Manor* was erected at Swindon Works in January 1938. Barcote Manor, which shared its name with the locomotive, was built in 1876 and is located not far from the site of the G.W.R's former workshop. By the early 1880s the building had been sold to William West, who was a director of the railway, and was inhabited by his family for a number of years. No. 7803 is pictured at Aberystwyth station's platform three on 7 July 1962 and the engine was withdrawn three years later in April 1965.

Above

Aberystwyth Station 2217

This scene was also captured at the beginning of July 1962, but features Collett '2251' Class 0-6-0 no. 2217. The locomotive was built at Swindon Works in June 1940 as one of 20 ordered in lot no. 337. As these engines were constructed during the Second World War the side windows in the cab were omitted to prevent light escaping at night and thus reduce the risk of enemy attack. The windows were subsequently fitted after the cessation of hostilities. No. 2217 is ready to depart from the Carmarthen branch platform with the 12.00 p.m. service. The platform currently serves trains of the narrow gauge Vale of Rheidol Railway.

Below
Aberystwyth Station 2217
No. 2217 was also captured by Bill arriving on the same day at Aberystwyth with the 8.43 a.m. service from Carmarthen. In the background, on the left-hand side, the station's engine shed and coal stage can be seen. The former had been built by the G.W.R. in 1938 and was a two-track through building, which replaced a similar structure dating from 1864, installed by the Aberystwith & Welsh Coast Railway. The shed closed in April 1965, but continued to be used by the steam locomotives of the Vale of Rheidol Railway until work recently began to upgrade the facilities. No. 2217 was condemned in November 1964.

Above
Ashford Works 7782
G.W.R. Collett '5700' Class 0-6-0PT engine no. 7782 stands on 'foreign' ground at Ashford Works with Southern Railway Maunsell N Class 2-6-0 no. 31414. No. 7782 was constructed by Armstrong Whitworth & Co. Ltd in November 1930 as one of only twenty-five members of the large '5700' Class to be built by the company. The picture was taken during the late 1950s to early 1960s and the engine would have been allocated to either Weymouth or Bristol Barrow Road depot. Withdrawal occurred in October 1964, while no. 31414 had left service just under two years earlier.

Opposite
Aberystwyth Station 7827
Aberystwyth station opened on 23rd June 1864 and was on the first section - from the town to Machynlleth - of the Aberystwith & Welsh Coast Railway to be completed. By 1865 the route had reached Barmouth and the company was taken over by Cambrian Railways a short time later. 'Manor' Class 4-6-0 no. 7827 *Lydham Manor* is seen here at the station with the 6.00 p.m. service to Whitchurch on the 17th August 1963. The engine was erected at Swindon Works in December 1950 and withdrawn in October 1965, but was saved from Woodham Brothers' Barry scrapyard in June 1970. The locomotive is currently operational on the Dartmouth Steam Railway.

Above

Barmouth Station 7313

No. 7313 was an example of G.J. Churchward's '4300' Class and the 2-6-0 was built at Swindon Works in December 1921. This year represented the mid-point in the construction of the class as it had begun in 1911 and continued to 1932 when 342 locomotives had been completed. No. 7313 has been modified to feature outside steam pipes and this occurred during mid-1958. The engine is pictured at Barmouth station with the 10.20 a.m. service to Ruabon.

Below
Barmouth Station 2204
No. 2204, of the '2251' Class, was constructed at Swindon Works in August 1939 and was in service until December 1963. The engine's last allocation was to Templecombe, after being at Machynlleth shed for Nationalisation. The engine is at the head of the 9.27 a.m. service to Pwllheli at Barmouth station; the train had originated from Ruabon. Barmouth station was opened by the A.&W.C.R. on 3rd June 1867, but was not reached by a locomotive until 10th October when a bridge to the station was given the all clear by the Board of Trade.

Opposite
Barmouth Station 2233
No. 2233, also belonging to the '2251' Class, has been captured at Barmouth station with the 10.25 a.m. Pwllheli to Dovey Junction service.

Opposite Below
Barmouth Station 3202
No. 3202 is seen arriving with the 9.00 a.m. Machynlleth to Barmouth passenger service. The engine was built at Swindon during October 1946 and was in service until August 1960 when withdrawn from Oswestry shed.

Below
Barmouth Station 3202
'2251' Class 0-6-0 no. 3202 leaves Barmouth Station later in the day with the 5.45 p.m., Sunday only, local service to Machynlleth.

Basingstoke Station 4908
G.W.R. Collett 'Hall' Class 4-6-0 no. 4908 *Broome Hall* is displaying an '81D' shedcode on the smokebox door, which meant that the engine was based at Reading depot. No. 4908 had arrived there from Penzance shed in March 1960, but only stayed at Reading a little over a year before being transferred to Oxford.

Basingstoke Station 4908
Broome Hall is again seen at Basingstoke. Two stations have served the town; the first was opened by the London & South Western Railway in June 1839, while the G.W.R's station, on the line from Reading, was completed in November 1848. The latter closed on 1st January 1932 and the former has been solely in use since.

Berkeley Road Station 1426
Pictured, arriving at Berkeley Road station with a service bound for Lydney, is G.W.R. '4800' Class, later '1400' Class, 0-4-2T locomotive no. 1426. The station was opened in July 1844 on the Bristol & Gloucester Railway line, but the connection to Lydney was not completed by the Severn & Wye Railway until 1879. A branch, forming part of the line, had been built by the Midland Railway, which was also part of the venture, and reached Sharpness first in 1876. Services to Lydney via the route ceased when part of the Severn Bridge collapsed in October 1960.

Left
Bodmin General Station 4552

G.W.R. Churchward '4500' Class 2-6-2T locomotive no. 4552 waits for the parcels to be loaded on to the train at Bodmin General station on 1st September 1960. The station was the terminus for the Bodmin branch line and has subsequently become the hub for the Bodmin & Wenford Steam Railway.

Left Bottom
Bodmin Road Station 4552

No. 4552 has also been pictured at Bodmin Road station and is ready to depart with a service to Bodmin General. The locomotive was constructed at Swindon Works during March 1915 and was withdrawn in September 1961.

Below
Bodmin Road Station 4565

Located on the Cornish main line, Bodmin Road station was opened almost two months after the route on 27th June 1859. The branch to Bodmin General was not installed until 27 May 1887 by the G.W.R. Bodmin Road was closed in January 1967 and the line followed in the early 1980s. No. 4565 is seen at the branch platform on 1st September 1960.

Opposite Top
Bourne End Station 1453
G.W.R. Collett '4800' Class 0-4-2T locomotive no. 1453 was built at Swindon Works in July 1937 as no. 4853. Renumbering of many members of the class occurred in 1946 and this engine was altered to no. 1453 in November.

Oppsite Bottom
Brent Station 4561
'4500' Class 2-6-2T no. 4561 is seen here at Brent Station's bay platform with the branch service to Kingsbridge. The South Devon Railway opened the station during June 1848, but the branch to Kingsbridge was added by the G.W.R. in December 1893. Both were victims of the Beeching Report in October 1964 and September 1963 respectively.

Below
Brecon Station 2218
Collett '2251' 0-6-0 no. 2218 has been photographed before departing with the 6.00 p.m. Brecon station to Hereford service on 21st April 1962. The engine was based at Ebbw Junction shed at this time, but would have spells at Westbury and Templecombe before withdrawal in November 1964.

Above
Bristol Bath Road Shed 7019
'Castle' Class 4-6-0 no. 7019 *Fowey Castle* was one of thirty locomotives built to Collett's design after Nationalisation. No. 7019 was erected at Swindon Works in May 1949 and was allocated to Bath Road from new until November 1961. The locomotive was one of a number of class members that acquired a double chimney in the late 1950s to early 1960s and *Fowey Castle* was equipped in September 1958.

Castle Caereinion Station Nos 822 and 823
The 2 ft 6 in. narrow gauge line between Welshpool and Llanfair Caereinion was opened by the Welshpool & Llanfair Light Railway on 4th April 1903 as an aid to transporting local people and the products of their businesses. However, use of the line by passengers was not great and these services were removed by the G.W.R. in February 1931. Goods services were sustained into the British Railways era, but by 3rd November 1956 these had also been discontinued. The Welshpool & Llanfair Light Railway Preservation Company Ltd was subsequently founded and leased the line from B.R. in 1962. The first service was operated between Llanfair Caereinion and Castle Caereinion on 6th April 1963. The two original 0-6-0T locomotives, no. 1 (G.W.R. no. 822) The Earl and no. 2 (G.W.R. no. 823) Countess, built by Beyer, Peacock & Co. Ltd in 1902, are seen at Castle Caereinion station on 17th August 1963. The line continues to thrive, having been subsequently extended to Welshpool, and the engines have been joined by a number of narrow gauge locomotives from around the world.

Opposite
Bristol Bath Road Shed 6957
Collett 'Hall' Class 4-6-0 no. 6957 *Norcliffe Hall* stands at Bristol Bath Road shed's ash pits. The engine was constructed at Swindon Works during April 1943 and was later allocated to the shed from May 1954 to October 1959. No. 6957 is fitted with an '82B' shed plate denoting St Phillips Marsh shed, which was the home of the locomotive from the latter date to February 1960, and Didcot, with shed code '81E', would house the engine until May 1961.

Above

Carmarthen Station 3693

Collett '8750' Class 0-6-0PT locomotive no. 3693 was built at Swindon in March 1941 as part of lot no. 330, which saw 50 engines produced between 1940 and 1942. After seeing in Nationalisation at Tyseley depot, no. 3693 moved to Swansea East Dock shed in May 1960 and followed this with a switch to Carmarthen in June 1961. The locomotive is pictured at Carmarthen station with the 12.35 p.m. to Llandeilo on 21st April 1962. No. 3693 subsequently transferred to Neath, July 1962, and Gloucester Horton Road, July 1963, before being condemned in July 1964.

Below
Carmarthen Station 5938
'Hall' Class locomotive no. 5938 *Stanley Hall* has been captured by Bill at Carmarthen station with the 8.00 a.m. Neyland to Paddington service on 21st April 1962. *Stanley Hall* was one of five 'Halls' constructed at Swindon Works during July 1933, the others comprising nos 5935-5937 and no. 5939. No. 5938 was allocated to Carmarthen shed for almost 10 years, arriving in September 1953 and departing during February 1963 for Ebbw Junction. Withdrawal from there occurred only a short time later in May 1963.

Cardiff Canton Shed 5096

No. 5096 *Bridgwater Castle* spent a year allocated to Cardiff Canton shed between September 1961 and September 1962; the engine has been pictured outside the six-track dead-end shed on 22nd April 1962. *Bridgwater Castle* relocated to Cardiff East Dock when Canton closed to steam on 10th September.

Cardiff Canton Shed 6004

Resting at the rear of Canton shed on 22nd April 1962 with B.R. Riddles 9F 2-10-0 no. 92203 was Collett 'King' Class 4-6-0 no. 6004 *King George III*. The locomotive was constructed at Swindon Works during July 1927 as part of lot no. 243 that comprised 20 engines. Whereas no. 92203 carried a double chimney from new, *King George III* had the arrangement fitted in July 1958. No. 6004 would only be in service for another two months after this photograph had been taken.

Cardiff Canton Shed 92220

B.R. 9F Class no. 92220 *Evening Star* is pictured at Canton shed's ash pits and behind the locomotive the carriage sheds are visible. No. 92220 was constructed at Swindon Works in March 1960 and named there on the 18th during a special ceremony, being the last engine to be built at the works, in addition to being the last steam locomotive to be erected for B.R. *Evening Star* was only in service for five years and then went into preservation as part of the national collection.

Cardiff Canton Shed 6847

The G.W.R. installed the shed facilities, located near Cardiff General station, in 1882. By the turn of the century a roundhouse had been attached to the building. 'Grange' Class 4-6-0 no. 6847 *Tidmarsh Grange* was completed at Swindon Works in October 1937 and

Cardiff Canton Shed 6003

'King' Class locomotive no. 6003 *King George IV* is depicted out of service with another 4-6-0 and a Churchward '5205' Class 2-8-0T, no. 5214, at Cardiff Canton shed on 22nd April 1962. No. 6003 was erected at Swindon Works in July 1927 and would be withdrawn from Cardiff in June 1962. No. 5214 left traffic from Aberbeeg in September 1964.

Cardiff Canton Shed 5261

Another Churchward '5205' Class 2-8-0T locomotive at Canton shed, on the same day as the above image, was no. 5261. The engine emerged from Swindon Works during February 1940 as part of the final batch of ten to replace a number of older members of the class which had been rebuilt as 2-8-2Ts. No. 5261 was allocated to Canton from December 1958 to September 1962.

Opposite Top
Chard Central Station 9670
Collett '8750' Class 0-6-0PT no. 9670 is awaiting departure with the Chard Central station service to Chard Junction on 12th August 1961. Chard Central was originally called Chard Joint when opened by the London & South Western Railway and Bristol & Exeter Railway on 11th September 1866 as the focal point for their respective branch lines to the town.

Opposite Bottom
Chard Central Station 3736
No. 3736 arrives at Chard Central station with the service from Taunton on the former B.&.E.R. line. 'Joint' was dropped from the station's name from March 1928, but 'Central' was not added until September 1949. Closure occurred on 10 September 1962. The locomotive was the first of eight '8750' Class engines built at Swindon in September 1937.

Below
Chard Junction Station 9663
Collett '8750' Class 0-6-0PT no. 9663 waits to leave with the Chard Junction station service to Chard Central station on 3rd September 1960. The former station was opened as Chard Road on 19th July 1860 by the L.&S.W.R., closing on 7th March 1966.

Opposite top
Chipping Norton Station 4100
Collett '5101' Class 2-6-2T no. 4100 was constructed at Swindon Works in August 1935. The class were a slightly modified version of the earlier '5100' Class engines and had frame alterations, outside steam pipes and increased coal capacity to four tons. No. 4100 is pictured at Chipping Norton station on 16th July 1962.

Opposite bottom
Chipping Norton Station 4100
No. 4100 is again seen on 16th July 1962, but with the 4.53 p.m. Chipping Norton to Kingham service. Passenger trains ceased running to Chipping Norton in December 1962 and the line had been pulled up by 1965; no. 4100 was withdrawn in October of that year.

Below
Cheltenham Spa St James Station 4101
G.W.R. '5101' Class locomotive no. 4101 was photographed at Cheltenham Spa St James station on 5th September 1962 with the 2.50 p.m. Cheltenham Spa St James station to Kingham passenger service. The former station was closed in January 1966 and the site has since been cleared, now being occupied by a supermarket. No. 4101 was withdrawn in June 1964 and scrapped.

Below

Clarbeston Road Station 9760

'8750' Class 0-6-0PT no. 9760 entered traffic from Swindon Works during September 1935. The class differentiated themselves from the earlier '5700' Class through altered cabs, boilers and other detail modifications. No. 9760 is portrayed at Clarbeston Road station with the 11.15 a.m. passenger service to Fishguard Harbour station on 21st April 1962. The locomotive was withdrawn from Duffryn Yard shed in December 1963.

Above

Churston Station 1466

Collett '1400' Class 0-4-2T engine no. 1466 stands at Churston station's bay platform for the Brixham branch with a passenger service to the town. The Dartmouth & Torbay Railway, which ran between the South Devon Railway at Torquay station (later renamed Torre) and Churston, was built in stages. The line did not open at the latter until 14th March 1861, after the completion of the first section in 1859. The last segment to Kingswear was ready in August 1864. Upon opening Churston was named Brixham Road and the change did not occur until 12th March 1868. This was only a short time after completion of the branch to Brixham, which was opened on 28th February by the Torbay & Brixham Railway. Further alterations to the station came at this time in the form of the addition of a bay platform. From 1st January 1973 the line has been operated solely by the Dart Valley Railway Co. and is now known as the Dartmouth Steam Railway. The Brixham branch closed in May 1963.

Above
Crewe South Shed 3815
The G.W.R. possessed a shed at Crewe called Gresty Lane, which was located on the
north side of the line to Nantwich and Shrewsbury, and this was constructed by the
London & North Western Railway in 1870, being subsequently leased to the G.W.R.
However, the shed was small and when at capacity visiting G.W.R. locomotives had to
seek space at the other Crewe depots. Collett '2884' Class 2-8-0 no. 3815 has found its
way to Crewe South shed during March 1960 and has the tender replenished by the
shed's mechanical coaler. The locomotive was allocated to Croes Newydd, Wrexham,
at this time and would be condemned while there in May 1964.

Opposite
Crewe North Shed 6859
'Grange' Class 4-6-0 no. 6859 *Yiewsley Grange* is pictured at the side of, a very
dilapidated, Crewe North shed and is flanked by two of B.R's Standard Class engines.
These are Standard Class Five no. 73131 and Standard Class Seven Pacific no. 70053
Moray Firth, while the tender of Thompson B1 Class 4-6-0 no. 61121 is visible between
the latter and no. 6859. Built at Swindon Works in December 1937, *Yiewsley Grange*
was in service until November 1965. No. 6859 has the '88A' shed code in place, but
in this instance the code refers to Cardiff East Dock shed which used the number
between September 1963 and July 1965. Cardiff Canton had applied the code to its
locomotives previously between 1961 and 1963.

Opposite top

Dulverton Station 7326

No. 7326, of the '7300' Class, has been photographed on 12th August 1961 travelling towards Taunton. Dulverton station's signal box and goods shed are the buildings behind the engine. The former was originally located a short distance away from the station on the west side of the line to Taunton. No. 7326 was allocated to the latter place from March 1961 until withdrawal in September 1963.

Opposite bottom

Dulverton Station 9765

No. 9765 was the last of six '8750' Class 0-6-0T engines to be built at Swindon during September 1935. The locomotive is on the west side of Dulverton station's island platform which accommodated trains bound for Exeter via the Exe Valley line. This route was open fully between May 1885 and October 1963.

Below

Dulverton Station 7337

Collett '9300', later '7300,' Class 2-6-0 no. 7337 is heading a goods train passing through Dulverton station. The '9300' Class were an updated version of the '4300' Class 2-6-0s and no. 7337 was erected at Swindon as no. 9315 in March 1932.

Above

Ellesmere Station 1458

This scene, dating from 11th June 1962, shows Collett 0-4-2T locomotive no. 1458 at the head of the 4.20 p.m. train from Ellesmere station to Wrexham Central station. The Oswestry, Ellesmere & Whitchurch Railway opened the former on 4th May 1863 as a terminus for the first section of line to be completed between Whitchurch and Ellesmere. The remainder of the route was not ready until July 1864 and just before this occasion the company amalgamated with several others to form the Cambrian Railways. Before the turn of the century Ellesmere was connected to Wrexham by a route backed by the Manchester, Sheffield & Lincolnshire Railway (later the Great Central Railway), but worked by the C.R. At the time of the picture this line would not be in operation for much longer as services ceased from 8th September 1962 and the track was then quickly removed. Ellesmere station closed on 18th January 1965, but the substantial station building, seen on the left (north side of the line), is still in existence.

Below

Exeter St David's Shed 7224

Collett '7200' Class 2-8-2T engine no. 7224 was rebuilt at Swindon Works in November 1935 from '5205' Class specifications. The locomotive was originally no. 5259 and completed in January 1926. For the conversion, the frames were lengthened at the rear to accommodate the rear axle and an larger coal bunker; the water tanks were also extended. No. 7224 is pictured two months into its six-month long allocation to Exeter St David's shed on 13th August 1961. The engine would move to Ebbw Junction at the end of the year and withdrawn from the depot in the following December.

Above
Exeter St David's Shed 5075
'Castle' Class locomotive no. 5075 was initially named *Devizes Castle* when built in August 1938. However, shortly after the start of the Second World War a number of the class were given the names of aircraft then being used by the Royal Air Force. No. 5075 became *Wellington* in October 1940. The locomotive is seen at Exeter St David's shed on 13th August 1961.

Opposite top
Exeter St David's Shed 1450
No. 1450 was based at Exeter from July 1962 to November 1963 and is seen at the shed, found on the north-west side of Exeter St David's station, on 24th February 1963.

Opposite bottom
Exeter St David's Shed 5564
Standing on an adjacent road to no. 1450 was '4575' Class 2-6-2T no. 5564. The shed was moved from it original position to the south in 1864 by the Bristol & Exeter Railway, who were builders of both structures. The new shed was a slightly larger through-track shed, but was extended further by the G.W.R. in 1894 and extensive improvements were also made to the facilities. Closure occurred in October 1963.

Opposite top
Exeter St David's Station 5049
A view of no. 5049 *Earl of Plymouth*. The locomotive entered traffic during May 1936 as *Denbigh Castle*. However, 15 months later, names of Earls intended for the Collett '3200' Class 4-4-0s were transferred to the 'Castle' Class and no. 5049 received *Earl of Plymouth*. The engine is displaying an '83A' shed code, which represents Newton Abbot, and *Earl of Plymouth* was based at the depot from July 1958 to April 1960.

Opposite bottom
Exeter St David's Station 6938
Collett 'Hall' no. 6938 *Corndean Hall* was constructed at Swindon Works during July 1942, but did not acquire its name until March 1946. The locomotive was also allocated to Newton Abbot and its stay lasted from January 1956 to November 1959. Withdrawal from Didcot occurred in March 1965.

Below
Exeter St David's Station 5049
'Castle' Class locomotive no. 5049 *Earl of Plymouth* rests at the head of an unidentified express in Exeter St David's station. The engine is paired with a straight-sided 4,000 gallon Hawksworth tender, which also had a six-ton coal capacity. The British Railways arms on the tender is the incorrect version which should be facing the opposite way.

Opposite top
Exeter St David's Station 5976
'Hall' Class 4-6-0 no. 5976 *Ashwicke Hall* was erected at Swindon Works in September 1938. After WWII the engine took part in G.W.R. oil burning experiments and this also led to a renumbering. No. 5976 was fitted in April 1947 and became no. 3951. However, this alteration was short-lived on *Ashwicke Hall* and a reversion was made to original specifications, and numbering, in November 1948.

Opposite bottom
Exeter St David's Station 5412
Collett '5400' Class 0-6-0PT locomotive no. 5412 was built at Swindon Works in May 1932. The engine is pictured at Exeter St David's on 30th August 1960 and would be withdrawn from Exeter shed in April 1962.

Below
Exeter St David's Station 4945
No. 4945 *Milligan Hall* was an early example of the 'Hall' Class and its completion took place in August 1929. The locomotive was one of a small number of the first eighty engines to have valve spindle crosshead guides omitted from its construction, but no. 4945 was in conformity with the other 'Halls' through having spring compensating beams fitted. *Milligan Hall* was a Westbury engine at the time of this picture.

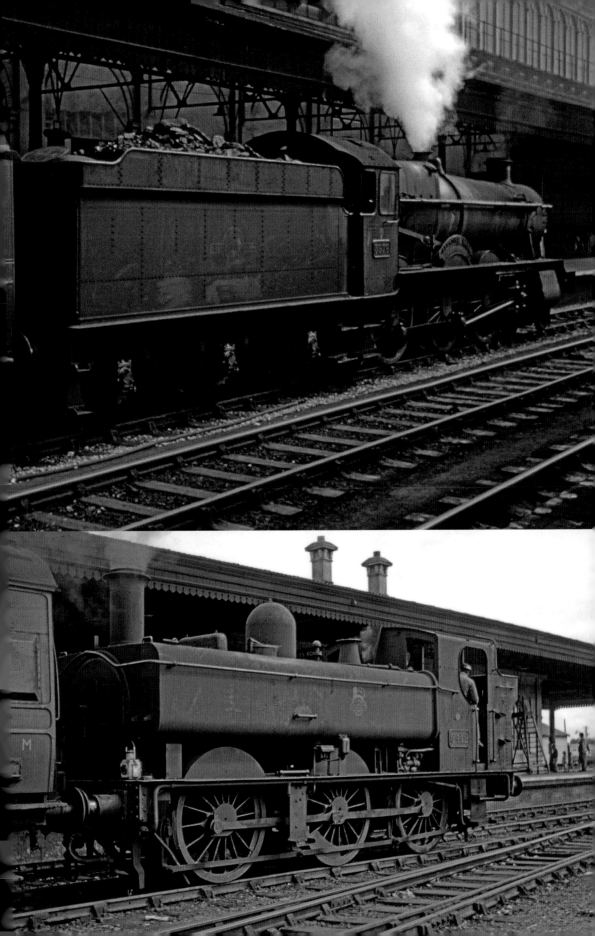

Above

Exeter St David's Station 5075

No. 5075 *Wellington* is at the head of 'The Royal Duchy' passenger service on 30th August 1960. The train had originated from London Paddington station and was destined for Penzance. *Wellington* was working from Exeter shed at this time and had arrived there from Plymouth Laira in June 1959. The locomotive would move on to Neath in July 1961 and then to Cardiff Canton and Bristol St Phillip's Marsh during its final nine months in service. Removal from traffic occurred during September 1962.

Below
Exeter St David's Station 5050
No. 5050 *Earl of St Germans* originally carried no. 5075's first name - *Devizes Castle* -when it entered service in May 1936. However, this was removed in August 1937 as the 'Earl' names were applied. No. 5050 stands across from St David's goods station on 13 August 1961 with an unidentified service. At this time the engine was working from Bristol St Phillip's Marsh depot and had recently arrived there, but the allocation would only last until the first month of 1962 when a four-month residency at Swindon began. *Earl of St Germans* then returned to St Phillip's Marsh and was condemned there in September 1963.

Below

Exeter St David's Station D800

Five Type Four diesel-hydraulic locomotives were ordered from the North British Locomotive Company in November 1955 by B.R. for use in the Western Region as part of the 'Pilot Scheme' for diesel locomotives to replace the steam fleet. However, Swindon Drawing Office staff were adamant that they could produce a suitable locomotive to the required specifications and successfully lobbied for prototypes of their own design to be produced. Whereas the N.B.L.C. units featured MAN engines and Voith transmission, the Swindon locomotives were equipped with 12-cylinder Maybach MD650 engines and Mekydro K104U 4-stage transmission. These were features of the Deutsche Bundesbahn V200 Class on which the new engines were based. The two engines of the three prototype locomotives were rated 1,035 hp at 1,400 rpm each, but for the production series this was increased to 1,135 hp at 1,530 rpm each. D800 entered traffic from Swindon Works in mid-1958 and was named *Sir Brian Robertson* after the Chairman of the British Transport Commission. Thirty-eight locomotives were built in total by Swindon, while thirty-three were ordered from the N.B.L.C. with their power units and transmission. These formed B.R. Classes 42 and 43 respectively, although all were referred to as the 'Warship' Class until the TOPS scheme was introduced as these formed the basis of the majority of the locomotives' names. D800 was only in service for ten years, but during this time the locomotive just fell short of running 1 million miles before withdrawal occurred in October 1968. This picture dates from 4th August 1967.

Above

Exeter St David's Station D820

Another Class 42 'Warship', D820 *Grenville,* has been captured on film at Exeter St David's Station in August 1967, with D806 *Cambrian* also present on the left. These pictures of the locomotives illustrate the livery changes applied to the class during their short careers. As new, the class entered service with the B.R. green livery applied (D800 has the early three-character route indicator box; these were later increased to four characters), but by the mid-1960s the W.R. decided to use maroon as the standard colour for its locomotives and over 30 'Warships' had the livery. Half-yellow cab fronts were also applied from the early 1960s before the entire front was painted in the colour. B.R. rail blue was introduced in 1965 and by the end of the following year a class member was transformed to this colour scheme. The 'Warships' were withdrawn between 1968 and December 1972; D820 was a casualty in November 1972, as was D806.

Above

Frome Shed 9615

During April 1958, Bill photographed '8750' 0-6-0PT locomotive no. 9615 outside the shed at Frome. This structure was located to the south of Frome station, on the west side of the line, and was 68 years old at this time, having been installed by the G.W.R. in 1890, replacing a similar building erected by the company in 1854. The shed would be closed by B.R. in September 1963 and subsequently removed: the imposing structure on the left was owned by E. Bailey & Son, producers of hops for the brewing industry, and has also since been demolished. No. 9615 was built at Swindon during September 1945 and was in service until July 1965. The engine was Westbury-allocated at the time of the picture.

Below

Falmouth Station 5537

In this photograph, Collett '4575' Class 2-6-2T locomotive no. 5537 has arrived at Falmouth station with the service from Truro. The engine had been erected at Swindon Works in July 1928 and was in service until August 1962. Falmouth station was opened on 24th August 1863 by the Cornwall Railway as the terminus for the company's broad gauge branch line from Truro. The C.R. became part of the G.W.R. in mid-1889 and the latter subsequently converted the gauge of the line in 1892. On the 7th December 1970 the station was closed and a new station opened to the west, being in closer proximity with the town. However, the original station was re-opened on 5th May 1975 and was later renamed Falmouth Docks station in October 1988.

Gloucester Horton Road Shed 5000

'Castle' Class 4-6-0 no. 5000 *Launceston Castle* is outside Gloucester shed on 22 April 1962. The engine emerged from Swindon Works in September 1926 and was one of fifteen locomotives built as part of lot no. 234 between 1926 and 1927. October 1964 saw no. 5000 taken out of service from Oxley depot.

Gloucester Horton Road Shed 7037

No. 7037 was the last 'Castle' Class locomotive to be erected in August 1950 and was later afforded the honour of carrying the name *Swindon*. The locomotive was named by Princess Elizabeth at Swindon Works in November 1950 and also carried the arms of the borough below the nameplates.

Gloucester Horton Road Shed 5068

No. 5068 *Beverston Castle* was visiting Gloucester from Swindon shed when this image was captured on 22nd April 1962. The engine had been a long-term resident at the latter, but its residency would soon come to an end as a transfer to Oxford transpired in May; withdrawal from the depot swiftly followed in September.

Gloucester Horton Road Shed 5000

Launceston Castle was also calling at Horton Road from Swindon shed. The locomotive had been allocated at the latter since November 1955, but would also be moved on in May, finding a new home at Gloucester Horton Road. By the end of 1962 no. 5000 had become a Hereford engine.

Gloucester Horton Road Shed 4929

'Hall' Class 4-6-0 no. 4929 *Goytrey Hall* is seen in Horton Road shed's yard on 22nd April 1962. The engine is in the company of War Department 'Austerity' 2-8-0 no. 90483 and classmate no. 4956 *Plowden Hall*. No. 4929 was constructed at Swindon in May 1929 and was in service until March 1965. A large proportion of the engine's later career was spent working from Horton Road depot.

Gloucester Horton Road Shed 7037
A view of the front end of no. 7037 *Swindon* taken while the tender is replenished with water.

Gloucester Horton Road Shed 5905
'Hall' no. 5905 *Knowsley Hall* was one of twenty locomotives constructed at Swindon as part of lot no. 275 in 1931. These engines were sent into traffic between May and August 1931; no. 5905 was ready in May and initially allocated to Westbury. The locomotive is now displaying an '87J' shedcode, which denoted a Fishguard Goodwick residency, and the engine would be on their roster until condemned in July 1963.

Below

Kemble Station 7010

Resting at the 'down' platform at Kemble station on 5th September 1962, perhaps with a service bound for Gloucester, was 'Castle' locomotive no. 7010 *Avondale Castle*. The G.W.R. opened the station on 12th May 1845 as part of the route between Swindon, Gloucester and Cheltenham Spa. However, at this time the station was only used for the exchange of passengers between the above route and the Cirencester branch line. Kemble station was made accessible to the general public on 1st May 1882 and until the turn of the century was known as Kemble Junction; the Tetbury branch was installed in 1889 and diverged from the main line here. The water tank seen behind the locomotive is still present at the station. No. 7010 was in service until March 1964.

Above

Gobowen Station 6945

No. 6945 *Glasfryn Hall* is photographed at Gobowen Station with the 12.20 p.m. Chester to Shrewsbury service. The route between these two places was opened by the Shrewsbury, Oswestry & Chester Junction Railway in 1848 and Gobowen station was first used on 14th October of that year. The locomotive was erected at Swindon during September 1942 and named four years later. When this image was captured *Glasfryn Hall* was working from Wolverhampton Stafford Road shed, but the locomotive would be withdrawn from Cardiff East Dock in September 1964.

Above

Kemble Station W79976

The Western Region acquired four railcars, nos W79975-W79978 with forty-six seats, from AC Cars Ltd in 1958 in readiness for the removal of steam services on the Tetbury and Cirencester branch lines in 1959. W79976 was the first to run on the Cirencester branch on 2nd February 1959 and at this time there were seventeen services to the town from Kemble station, while to Tetbury and back, nine services operated. W79976 is seen at Kemble station with a service for Tetbury of 5th September 1962. The branch lines were subsequently closed from 6th April 1964 and the railcars were re-deployed; W79976 went to the Southern Region first and then the Scottish Region before withdrawal in January 1968. The railcar has been earmarked for preservation a number of times, but these have not come to fruition and the body shell has been stored at the Great Central Railway, Loughborough, for a number of years.

Opposite

Leamington Spa Station 5067

'Castle' Class 4-6-0 no. 5067 *St Fagans Castle* has stopped at Leamington Spa station during May 1961 with a service bound for London. The engine was constructed in July 1937 and was subsequently based at Old Oak Common shed, Swindon, Bristol Bath Road and Carmarthen. No. 5067 had recently transferred to Reading and would leave service from the depot during the following July.

Leamington Spa Station 5019

'Grange' Class 4-6-0 no. 6855 *Saighton Grange* is assisted by 'Castle' no. 5019 *Treago Castle* at Leamington Spa station during May 1961. The engines were working from Tyseley and Wolverhampton Stafford Road depots respectively.

Leamington Spa Station 5057
Another 'Castle' at Leamington Spa. No. 5057 *Earl of Waldegrave* was *Penrice Castle* between June 1936 and October 1937. The engine is also paired with a Hawksworth straight-side tender and this was one of several pairings with this type during the locomotive's career.

Leamington Spa Station 6011
'King' Class 4-6-0 no. 6011 *King James I* entered service from Swindon Works in April 1928. The locomotive has been modified in two respects since that time. 'Alfloc' water treatment apparatus was fitted in 1954 and then in March 1956 a double chimney was added.

Above

Leamington Spa Station 6007

Two 'King' Class locomotives have carried no. 6007 and name *King William III*. The first was built at Swindon in March 1928, but was damaged beyond repair after a collision with detached coal wagons at Shrivenham on 15th January 1936. A replacement engine was competed in March 1936 and continued working until September 1962.

Below

Liskeard Station 5539

Collett '4575' Class 2-6-2T locomotive no. 5539 was erected at Swindon in July 1928. A modification carried out subsequently, and visible here, was the fitting of a curved plate at the bunker top to surround the top lamp iron which transpired some time during the late 1930s to early 1940s. No. 5539 has stopped at Liskeard station with a service from Looe. The stations were opened on 4th May 1859 and 11th September 1879 respectively, but they were not connected until 15th May 1901 when an extension was built from Moorswater, to the west of Liskeard.

Above
Lostwithiel Station 8733
Manoeuvring freight at Lostwithiel station is '5700' Class 0-6-0PT locomotive no. 8733. Constructed by W.G. Bagnall Ltd in March 1931, the engine was in service until February 1962.

Opposite top
Liskeard Station D6320 and D6315
B.R. Type Two, later Class 22, diesel-hydraulic locomotives D6320 and D6315 leave Liskeard station with a Penzance to Plymouth express passenger service. Six were initially ordered as part of the Pilot Scheme, but before these entered service a further 52 were authorised and to be produced by the N.B.L.C. D6320 was completed in March 1960, while D6315 was in traffic by January 1960. Both were initially worked from Plymouth Laira shed and the class were generally used in pairs until the arrival of the more powerful Class 42 and 43 locomotives.

Opposite bottom
Llandeilo Station 3693
'8750' Class 0-6-0PT locomotive no. 3693 has been pictured at Llandeilo station on 21st April 1962 with the 3.23 p.m. passenger service to Carmarthen.

Above

Lostwithiel Station 1419

Collett '1400' Class 0-4-2T locomotive no. 1419 is waiting patiently for the departure time of the Lostwithiel station service to Fowey on 1st September 1960. Lostwithiel station was opened by the Cornwall Railway on 4th May 1859, while the Fowey branch was completed to Carne Point just 10 years later by the Lostwithiel & Fowey Railway. The five-mile long branch was built for mineral purposes, namely to transport china clay from local quarries to the harbour near Fowey. The competing Cornwall Minerals Railway opened an alterative route from Par in 1874 and the company subsequently built Fowey station and introduced passenger services on 20th June 1876. The L.&F.R. encountered financial difficulties around this time and was later dissolved and then bought by the C.M.R., who made a number of improvements, including a connection to Fowey station, and re-opened the line in September 1895. Passenger services were stopped briefly during the two world wars, but they were later removed entirely as Fowey station closed on 4th January 1965. The line from Par had been lifted by the end of the decade, but the route from Lostwithiel is still used by mineral trains. No. 1419 was built in November 1933 and withdrawn in April 1961.

Below
Minehead Station 5522
'4575' Class 2-6-2T no. 5522 was built at Swindon Works in December 1927 as part of lot no. 249. The engine was present at Taunton shed for Nationalisation and, apart from a brief sojourn at Exeter in 1953, carried out its duties from the depot until removed from service in March 1959. No. 5522 has been photographed by Bill at Minehead station with a local service to Taunton. The former station was opened on 16th July 1874 by the Minehead Railway as the terminus for an extension from Watchet and the West Somerset Railway Co. line to Taunton, which was operated by the B.&E.R. Minehead was closed by B.R. on 4th January 1971, but in 1976 the station re-opened as part of a heritage railway operated by the West Somerset Railway Plc.

Below
Newton Abbot Shed 6002
'King' Class 4-6-0 no. 6002 *King William IV* rests on the west side of the Newton Abbot shed and works site (east side of Newton Abbot station) on 2nd September 1960. The works, for locomotive erection and repairs, in addition to the maintenance of carriages, was installed by the South Devon Railway and continued in the capacity of a repair facility after the G.W.R. absorbed the company in the early 1890s. The original two-track shed was closed at this time and a six-track building was built on to the south end of the works. This was open until 1962 when it was converted to a diesel shed, but final closure occurred in the 1980s. The repair works have since become the centre of an industrial estate and house a propeller manufacturer for the maritime industry. No. 6002, built at Swindon in July 1927, was in service until September 1962.

Above

Newquay Station 3635

No. 3635, of the '8750' Class. was the first engine of lot no. 325 to be constructed at Swindon in September 1939. The order was not completed until July 1940 and no. 3684 was the last of the lot to enter traffic. No. 3635 has been photographed at Newquay station's platform one with the service from Chacewater. At the latter, the Newquay to Truro line intersected the Plymouth to Penzance route. The former was completed by the G.W.R. in 1905 from Blackwater Junction near Chacewater to Shepherds were it connected with the existing Treamble branch line from Newquay. The Newquay to Truro line was opened for a relatively short period as it closed in February 1963. No. 3635 was condemned to be scrapped in April 1965.

Above

Newton Abbot Station 7029

Collett '5100' Class 2-6-2T no. 5153 reverses to form a connection with 'Castle' Class engine no. 7029 *Clun Castle*, which presumably needs assistance with its express passenger service. No. 7029 was built at Swindon in May 1950 and the locomotive's first allocation was to Newton Abbot depot; this lasted 12 years. The photograph dates from before October 1959 when the engine would undergo a number of modifications during its third general repair. *Clun Castle* received a double chimney and four-row superheater with 28 flues, in addition to a Hawksworth straight-sided tender. No. 7029 left service from Gloucester Horton Road in December 1965, after having the honour of taking the last steam service out of London Paddington station in June. *Clun Castle* was subsequently bought for preservation and is currently under overhaul at Tyseley Locomotive Works.

Opposite

Newton Abbot Station 5920

'Hall' no. 5920 *Wycliffe Hall* is ready to continue its journey with a 'down' express from Newton Abbot station. The engine was manufactured at Swindon Works during August 1931 and was the last locomotive to enter traffic without a compartment to store the fire irons. No. 5920 was also the penultimate member of the class to have the top lamp iron fitted above the smokebox door as the following locomotives had it fitted to the door; the earlier engines were subsequently altered to conform. *Wycliffe Hall* has the '83A' shed code and the engine was allocated to Newton Abbot depot from 1950 to 1959. Transfers to Taunton and Westbury occurred before no. 5920 left traffic in January 1962.

Above

Newton Abbot Station 5153

No. 5153 stands in front of no. 7029 at Newton Abbot station. This was opened by the South Devon Railway 31st December 1846 as Newton station and was on the company's line from Exeter. The station became known as Newton Abbot from 1st March 1877, just over a year after the S.D.R. had been absorbed by the G.W.R., and was later rebuilt, re-opening during April 1927. The locomotive entered traffic from Swindon in March 1930 and was at work until November 1964. At the time of the photograph the engine was Newton Abbot-allocated and this residency lasted from March 1959 to September 1962.

Opposite

Newton Abbot Station 1000

In the early 1940s, F.W. Hawksworth produced a design for a new two-cylinder 4-6-0 which incorporated a number of progressive features. These included; plate frames, high pressure boiler working at 280 psi (however, from 1956 this was reduced to 250 psi) with a high degree of superheat, 6 ft. 3 in. diameter coupled wheels, continuous splashers and straight-sided tenders. Thirty locomotives to the design were constructed at Swindon between 1945 and 1947 and no. 1000 was the first to enter traffic in August of the former year. The locomotives were designated the '1000' or 'County' Class as the engines were subsequently bestowed with names derived from those served by the railway; no. 1000 was christened *County of Middlesex* in March 1946. The locomotive is pictured at Newton Abbot with an express service on 4th August 1958 and at this time no. 1000 was working from Bristol Bath Road shed. In July 1964 *County of Middlesex* was taken out of traffic while based at Swindon depot.

Above
Old Oak Common Shed 'Blue Pullman'
The diesel-electric 'Blue Pullman' trains were introduced in 1960 and built by Metropolitan-Cammell. A total of five units were constructed by the company for use on the London - Manchester, London - Birmingham and London - Bristol services. Two sets were used by the London Midland Region and these consisted of six vehicles, while the remainder were utilised on the Western Region and comprised eight cars. This unidentified eight-vehicle set awaits its next duty at Old Oak Common shed.

Opposite below
Newton Abbot Station D839
'Warship' Class locomotive D839 *Relentless* is at Newton Abbot station on 3 August 1967.
Below
Old Oak Common Shed 7029
Clun Castle was captured by Bill on Sunday, 31st March 1963 when the engine was allocated to Old Oak Common shed. The stay here lasted two years three months after transfer from Newton Abbot depot had occurred in July 1962.

Old Oak Common Shed 7008

No. 7008 *Swansea Castle* worked for B.R. until September 1964. For the last 18 months of its career, the locomotive belonged to Old Oak Common and during this time would have witnessed the beginning of the conversion of the facilities to cater for the growing number of diesel locomotives; Type Four, later Class 47, diesel-electric locomotive D1696 lurks in the background of this photograph.

Oxford Station 6147
Collett '6100' Class 2-6-2T locomotive no. 6147 is pictured from the 'down' platform at Oxford station looking northwards. The engine was constructed at Swindon Works in January 1933 and was in service until December 1965.

Oxford Station 6147
Another view of no. 6147 at Oxford. The station was opened by the G.W.R. on 12th June 1844 as the terminus for a branch from the company's London to Bristol line at Didcot. However, the station was later replaced by an open-ended facility when the line was extended to Banbury.

Above

Oxford Shed 2892

Collett '2884' Class 2-8-0 no. 2892 has been positioned in front of no. 7404 in the same sidings at Oxford shed. In 1938 Collett introduced a modernised version of Churchward's '2800' Class 2-8-0s and no. 2892 was one of the first engines of the class to be built at Swindon in April 1938. The '2884' Class, which eventually totalled 83 when the last entered traffic in 1942, were different from their predecessors in having altered frame and motion plates, side window cabs, outside steam pipes and Automatic Train Control apparatus. No. 2892 was allocated to Severn Tunnel Junction depot at Nationalisation, but soon afterwards moved to Cardiff Canton. The engine returned to the former shed in February 1959 and is displaying its depot code in the picture. No. 2892 was taken out of traffic in May 1963 to be scrapped.

Opposite

Oxford Shed 7404

Collett '7400' Class 0-6-0PT no. 7404 sits, removed from the action, at Oxford shed, which was located just to the north of Oxford station on the west side of the line. The coal bunker has 'All Out. W.O. Thur' scrawled in chalk which could indicate that the boiler was empty in anticipation of a wash out. The locomotive was completed at Swindon Works in August 1936 and was allocated to Weymouth when new, but no. 7404 had found its way to Oxford for Nationalisation and was resident at the depot for the majority of the time it was a servant of B.R. The engine's final move was to Swansea East Dock shed and this took up the period beginning December 1963 to withdrawal during June 1964. St Barnabas Church tower is seen in the background with the original campanile roof which has since had the pitch greatly reduced.

Above
Oxford Station 7412
Pictured at an unidentified location around Oxford station during September 1960 is '7400' Class 0-6-0PT no. 7412. The class were a variation of the '5400' Class and differed through reduced diameter coupled wheels, higher boiler pressure and a lack of auto-train apparatus. No. 7412 was erected at Swindon in December 1936 and was in service until July 1963 when withdrawn from Oxford shed. The engine had been allocated there during the 1950s after seeing the end of the G.W.R. at Fairford.

Opposite
Oxford Station 6947
'Hall' Class engine no. 6947 *Helmingham Hall* pauses at Oxford station with an express freight service. The locomotive was the second of five 'Halls' to be completed in December 1942 and it was also the second to be named after the war, the *Helmingham Hall* nameplates being fitted during November 1946. During the B.R. period, allocations to Worcester and Gloucester occurred before no. 6947 arrived at Oxford depot in mid-1965. The stay was only brief, however, as by November *Helmingham Hall* had been removed from service.

Below

Paddington Station 6169

Collett '6100' Class 2-6-2T no. 6169 is running light engine at Paddington station during the late 1950s to early 1960s. The locomotive was the last of the class to enter traffic from Swindon in November 1935 after construction of the engines had begun in April 1931; the only year not to witness the completion of a '6100' Class locomotive was 1934. The main difference from the '5101' Class engines, on which the class were based, was an increase in the boiler pressure by 25 psi from 200 psi with a consequent rise in the tractive effort by 3,040 lb to 27,340 lb. No. 6169 was allocated to Southall depot for a number of years before a transfer to Old Oak Common transpired in November 1960. The locomotive was briefly at Cardiff Radyr shed and the final 16 months of its career were spent working from Worcester. No. 6169 was condemned for scrap in October 1965.

Above

Paddington Station 9412

Hawksworth '9400' Class 0-6-0PT no. 9412 brings empty coaching stock into Paddington station. The locomotive was the third member of the class to be erected for British Railways by Robert Stephenson & Hawthorns Ltd at the company's Newcastle works. Only ten of the class had been built for the G.W.R. before Nationalisation and these were different from the 200 locomotives erected for B.R. through being equipped with superheaters. No. 9412 went into traffic at Barry shed in March 1950. However, by May 1951 Old Oak Common depot had received the engine and it was based there for the next ten years. A number of the '9400' Class locomotives worked in the London area and one of their principal duties was the movement of coaching stock to and from Paddington. No. 9412 saw out its career at Neath and was withdrawn in March 1963.

Below
Par Station 5028
Plymouth Laira-allocated 'Castle' no. 5028 *Llantilio Castle* has been pictured by Bill at Par station on 4th August 1958. The service is unidentified, but 'The Cornishman' headboard is visible on the right-hand side of the smokebox, indicating that the locomotive could have been at the head of the train, which had originated from Wolverhampton, earlier in the day and is returning to Plymouth with another service. No. 5028 was built at Swindon in May 1934 and spent four years at Laira before moving on, but later returned in June 1956. The locomotive otherwise worked from Newton Abbot, with just a brief tenure at Truro forming the remainder of *Llantilio Castle*'s allocation history.

Above

Par Station 5538

Par station, opened by the Cornwall Railway on 4th May 1859, was later joined by Par St Blazey station, which was installed by the Cornwall Minerals Railway in June 1876 on their line to Newquay. During October 1877 the latter was leased by the G.W.R. and a connection between the two stations was made, opening at the start of 1879. The C.M.R. was taken over by the G.W.R. in mid-1896 and the latter subsequently improved the Newquay line by adding another track in the 1920s and 1930s. Collett '4545' Class 2-6-2T locomotive no. 5538 stands at Par station with a Newquay service. The locomotive was constructed at Swindon in July 1928 and was in service until October 1961.

Above

Penzance Shed 1028

Resting in front of no. 7812 at Penzance shed on 1st September 1960 was Hawksworth 'County' Class 4-6-0 no. 1028 *County of Warwick*. Evidently, the locomotive has, or is prepared to take charge of 'The Cornishman' service. This train service originated in the late 1800s and ran between London Paddington and Penzance until the early 1900s before being revived in the early 1950s, but in this instance the train began its journey at Wolverhampton. No. 1028 entered service in March 1947 and was a Bristol Bath Road engine from this time until the shed closed in September 1960; the engine is still fitted with the '82A' shed code. No. 1028 has been altered from its original condition through being equipped with a double chimney. The class acquired this equipment between 1956 and 1959, with *County of Warwick* being a recipient in August 1958.

Opposite

Penzance Shed 7812

'Manor' Class 4-6-0 no. 7812 *Erlestoke Manor* has been photographed on 1st September 1960 at Penzance Long Rock shed and the engine stands on a track at the south end of the depot. *Erlestoke Manor* was erected as part of the first lot, no. 316, of 20 locomotives, which were completed between 1938 and 1939, and these engines incorporated components, such as the coupled wheels, taken from withdrawn Churchward '4300' Class 2-6-0s, with a new lightweight boiler. No. 7812 entered traffic during January 1939 and was one of three to have Bristol Bath Road as their first depot. By the time this picture was taken, no. 7812 was on the cusp of a transfer to Oswestry shed after a brief period working from Truro. *Erlestoke Manor* spent its final two years in traffic working from Shrewsbury and was condemned there in November 1965. Subsequently, the locomotive was rescued from Woodham Bros Barry scrapyard and returned to service on the Severn Valley Railway in 1979. No. 7812 is currently still at work on the railway.

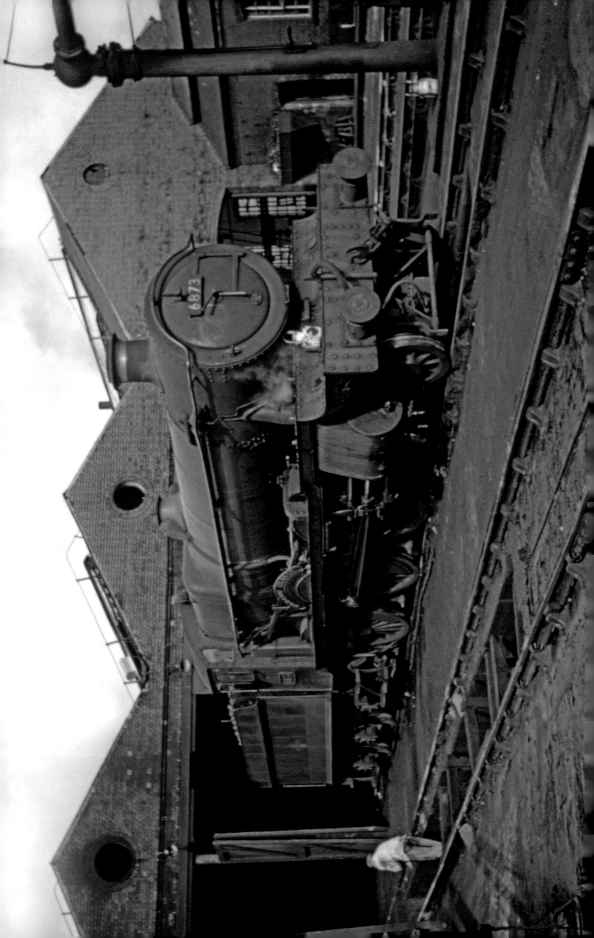

Above

Penzance Shed 8473

'9400' Class 0-6-0PT engine no. 8473 appears to have been abandoned on a siding at Penzance shed. Fifty members of the class were constructed by the Yorkshire Engine Co., Sheffield, between 1949 and 1956, and twenty of these had been sub-contracted from Hunslet Engine Co., who could not fulfil the original order because of other obligations. No. 8473 was built in August 1951 as part of the original order for thirty placed at the Yorkshire Engine Co. in 1948. Vernon (2008) records that the order for these locomotives more than doubled the company's revenue for new construction and they were the only engines of the class from private contractors which did not require the valves being re-set upon arrival at Swindon. No. 8473 was allocated to Penzance depot from new and was condemned there in January 1961.

Opposite

Penzance Shed 6873

A number of depots have been installed at Penzance to service and stable locomotives. The first was a one-track shed located next to the station and was in use for the West Cornwall Railway between 1852 and 1876. The company opened a second two-road facility to the north, on the west side of the line, in 1866, but this also closed in 1876 as the G.W.R. took over the railway and erected their own two-track depot just to the south of the 1866 shed. This was in use until 1914 when the Long Rock depot was built a mile to the east of the site of the aforementioned depots and it had four roads and a repair shop. 'Grange' Class 4-6-0 no. 6873 *Caradoc Grange* stands outside the shed on 1st September 1960. The engine was the first of five (6873-6877) 'Granges' to be built at Swindon in April 1939 and the final two would be completed in May bringing the class total to 80 locomotives. No. 6873 was predominantly allocated to Plymouth Laira shed during the B.R. period, but did work for a month from Penzance between December 1958 and January 1959. Withdrawal from Bristol St Phillip's Marsh occurred in June 1964.

Above

Penzance Shed 6808

Another 'Grange' present at Penzance on 1st September 1960 was no. 6808 *Beenham Grange*. The locomotive was built in September 1936 and its first allocation was to Penzance shed; this was also the case for the first member of the class, no. 6800 *Arlington Grange*. Both engines would have a long association with the shed for the remainder of their careers. *Beenham Grange* had moves to Cardiff East Dock, Llanelly and Oxley in the early 1960s before withdrawal in August 1964.

Opposite

Penzance Shed 6860

'Grange' Class 4-6-0 no. 6860 *Aberporth Grange* is seen here on the south side of Penzance engine shed next to the turntable, which was adjacent to sidings and the line to Penzance station. The locomotive saw a number of transfers around the Western Region during the B.R. period and this included two spells at Penzance. The first lasted from December 1953 to August 1955, while the second was from December 1955 to October 1960 and as this picture dates from 1st September 1960 a move to Llanelly was imminent. *Aberporth Grange* was in service for a further five years and was condemned at Cardiff East Dock depot in February 1965.

Below

Penzance Shed 6824

'Grange' Class locomotive no. 6824 *Ashley Grange* was the last of five class members to be constructed at Swindon Works in January 1937. At Nationalisation the engine was based at Carmarthen, but by February 1952 no. 6824 was a resident at Penzance and this lasted until August 1962. *Ashley Grange* was later withdrawn from Oxford depot in April 1964. Penzance shed was closed to steam engines by B.R. on 10th September 1962 as diesel locomotives took over use of the facilities. The shed was closed in mid-1976 and subsequently demolished to provide space for a new diesel depot, sidings and associated facilities.

Above

Penzance Station 6855

No. 6855 *Saighton Grange* has been photographed at the head of 'The Cornishman' service at Penzance station during August 1958. The 'Grange' Class featured; 5 ft 8 in. diameter coupled wheels, 5 ft 6 in. diameter boiler tapering to 4 ft 10$\frac{13}{16}$ in. working at 225 psi with 176 2 in. diameter small tubes, 14 5$\frac{1}{8}$ in. diameter superheater flues and 84 1 in. diameter superheater elements, and 2 cylinders 18½ in. diameter by 30 in. stroke with 9 in. piston valves. No. 6855 was in service from November 1937 until October 1965. At the time of the picture *Saighton Grange* was working from Plymouth.

Below

Penzance Station 7909

Also pictured at Penzance station in August 1958 was 'Modified Hall' Class locomotive no. 7909 *Heveningham Hall*. After assuming the C.M.E's position in 1941, Hawksworth sought to update the design for new 'Hall' Class engines, of which 71 were subsequently constructed at Swindon between 1944 and 1950. These locomotives featured plate frames, for the main set and the bogie, new cylinders and smokebox saddle, which were now manufactured separately and bolted together. Further, a new boiler was designed to incorporate a larger superheater with 21 5⅛ in. diameter flues and 84 1¼ in. elements, as opposed to 14 5⅛ in. diameter flues and 84 1 in. diameter superheater elements in the Collett 'Hall' boilers. No. 7909 *Heveningham Hall* was built in January 1950 and was in service until November 1965. At the time of this image, the engine was coming to the end of an eight-year stay at Plymouth depot.

Above

Penzance Station 5028

'Castle' no. 5028 *Llantilio Castle* was also seen by Bill at Penzance station's platform two, with a number of other admirers, during August 1958. The locomotive was less than two years away from being condemned and was one of the earliest 'Castle' Class withdrawals, apart from the engines rebuilt from earlier classes to the specifications. *Llantilio Castle*'s early demise was due to a collision with B.R. Type Four 'Warship' Class diesel-hydraulic locomotive D602 *Bulldog* at Davenport Junction near Plymouth station on 16th December 1959. The latter locomotive had brought the 10.30 p.m. Paddington to Penzance sleeping car service to the aforementioned station where it was relieved by no. 5028. *Bulldog* departed first and failed at Davenport Junction fouling the main line in such a way as to not alert the nearby signal box to the danger and causing the collision. Both locomotives were damaged, but there were no serious injuries to the passengers or footplatemen. D602 was repaired and returned to traffic but no. 5028 was condemned in May 1960.

Above

Penzance Station 6836

Penzance station was opened by the West Cornwall Railway on 11th March 1852 as the terminus for the line between the town and Truro. The line made use of the existing Hayle Railway route, which was a mineral railway opened in the late 1830s, between Redruth and Hayle. The station was originally a timber structure, but this was later replaced by a more substantial composition in the 1870s after the W.C.R. had become part of the G.W.R., which also updated other sections of the system. 'Grange' Class engine no. 6836 *Estevarney Grange* entered traffic in September 1937 and left service in August 1965. Working from Newton Abbot at the time of this picture of the locomotive, which was taken at Penzance station's platform one, no. 6836 would be condemned at Worcester.

Opposite

Penzance Station 5021

'Castle' no. 5021 *Whittington Castle* was also on view at Penzance station's platform two; the engine is at the head of an unidentified express passenger service. The locomotive was built at Swindon in August 1932 and worked from Plymouth Laira until the mid-point of the decade when moves between the depot and Newton Abbot occurred. By 1939 *Whittington Castle* was working close to its namesake after a transfer to Shrewsbury shed. The engine remained in the area (also having spells at Wolverhampton Stafford Road) until mid-1948 when it returned to south west England. The last three years of the locomotive's service life were spent at Cardiff Canton and Bristol St Phillip's Marsh and withdrawal occurred at the former in September 1962.

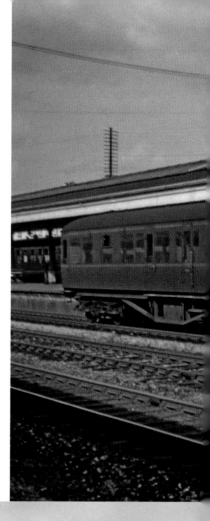

Below
Plymouth Station 4591
Collett '4575' Class 2-6-2T locomotive no. 4591 is at the east end of Plymouth station, with Apsley Road visible in the background. The '4575' Class was a development of Churchward's '4500' Class engines through an increase in the capacity of the water tanks from 1,000 gallons to 1,300 gallons. A total of 100 locomotives were erected to the former design and no. 4591 was completed in March 1927. The engine has subsequently been modified by acquiring a sliding shutter for the cab opening. After a number of spells working from Plymouth Laira shed, no. 4591 was withdrawn from Swindon in August 1964. The station was opened on 28th March 1877 as Plymouth North Road by the G.W.R. and London & South Western Railway. From the 15th September 1958 the station has been known as just Plymouth.

Above

Princes Risborough 6421

Collett '6400' Class 0-6-0PT locomotive no. 6421 is seen with a branch passenger train at Princes Risborough station on 17th September 1960. The first station to service the town was opened by the Wycombe Railway on 1st August 1862 on the line between High Wycombe and Thame. The line was operated by the G.W.R. and the company had acquired the W.R. by the end of the 1860s. By the beginning of the 20th century the G.W.R. had formed a partnership with the Great Central Railway to improve their respective networks in the area and this resulted in the improvement of the above section of track and the facilities at Princes Risborough. A new station, just to the south of the first, was inaugurated on 2nd April 1906, accommodating trains bound for the capital, the midlands or the Watlington and Aylesbury branches. No. 6421 was erected at Swindon in August 1935 and was condemned at Plymouth in February 1963. In September 1960 the engine was working from Banbury and would move to Wolverhampton Wellington depot just over a year later before reporting for its final allocation.

Above
Princes Risborough 1473

Also photographed on 17th September 1960 at Princes Risborough station was Collett '1400' Class engine no. 1473 and it is in charge of a service to Aylesbury. The engine was the penultimate member of the class to be erected and entered traffic in April 1936 as no. 4873. Construction of the '4800' Class had begun in August 1932 to replace '517' Class locomotives of the same wheel arrangement which were being dispensed with. The '4800' Class were based on the latter class, but brought into line with modern practices and eventually numbered 75 members. No. 1473 worked initially from Chippenham, but at Nationalisation the locomotive was based at Banbury as no. 1473 after being renumbered in November 1946. From November 1953 to January 1961, the ex-G.C.R. and London and North Eastern Railway depot at Neasden housed the engine and withdrawal occurred at Gloucester Horton Road in August 1962.

Below
Princes Risborough 6147
Two years after completion of the W.R. line between High Wycombe and Thame, the company extended its route from the latter to Kennington Junction just south of Oxford on the G.W.R's line from Didcot. Arriving at Princes Risborough station with a local service to Oxford was '6100' Class 2-6-2T no. 6147, which has also been captured entering the city's station by Bill on page 83. The locomotive was a long-term Southall shed resident until 1960 when it underwent four transfers in five years. These were Bristol St Phillip's Marsh during December 1960, Bristol Barrow Road in November 1962, Westbury a year later and finally Worcester in January 1964.

Below
Princes Risborough 1473
Another view of Collett '1400' Class locomotive no. 1473 at Princes Risborough station on 17th September 1960. The engine is coupled to autocoach W172W.

Above

Princes Risborough 6150

Departing from Princes Risborough station on 17th September 1960 was another '6100' Class locomotive, no. 6150. Seventy members of the class were constructed in total and forty of these entered traffic with Automatic Train Control Apparatus; no. 6150 conformed in this respect when it was built at Swindon in February 1933. The engine worked from Oxford Shed for a time in the early 1960s and was later condemned at Didcot depot in March 1965.

Below
Princes Risborough 5420
Photographed at the station with a local branch service in September 1960 was Collett 0-6-0PT locomotive no. 5420 of the '5400' Class. The early engines were the forebears of the later '6400' and '7400' Classes, but the former were primarily intended to work local passenger services. To aid them in this sphere, the locomotives were equipped with 5 ft 2 in. diameter coupled wheels and an auto-train capability. No. 5420 was the first engine of the last batch of five engines, lot no. 301, to be constructed at Swindon between November and December 1935. The first twenty '5400' Class locomotives were sent into traffic between November 1931 and June 1932, excluding the prototype which was rebuilt to the specifications and tested between August 1930 and June 1932 before being scrapped. No. 5420 had a much longer lifespan and was in service until October 1963, at which time the engine was condemned at Gloucester Barnwood depot.

Above

Radley Station 1435

During September 1960 Bill visited Radley station and took this image of '1400' Class locomotive no. 1435 with a branch passenger service to Abingdon. The station was opened on 8th September 1873 to replace an exchange only station for the Abingdon branch called Abingdon Junction. The Abingdon Railway Company had constructed the line and the facilities 17 years earlier, opening 2nd June 1856 from the G.W.R's Didcot to Oxford line. The latter company operated the line and subsequently acquired the A.R.C. in 1904. No. 1435 was built in August 1934 and began its career not too far away at Stourbridge shed. By the time this picture was taken the engine had reached Oxford and would end its service life there in January 1962. Passenger services on the Abingdon branch ceased on 9th September 1963, but goods traffic, in the form of vehicle trains from the nearby M.G. car factory, kept the route in use until June 1984.

Below

St Ives Station 4554

The G.W.R. completed the installation of a route from St Erth on the Penzance line to a terminus at St Ives on 1st June 1877. Also erected at this time was a stone engine shed with one track and coal and water facilities. The shed and water tank are visible to the left of '4500' Class 2-6-2T locomotive no. 4554, which is seen with an unidentified service at St Ives station. The engine was the last of lot no. 201 to be turned out from Swindon, being completed in March 1915. This batch were the first of the class to be built with superheaters and these consisted of 6 5⅛ in. flues and 48 ⅞ in. diameter elements. Later, the superheaters used by these locomotives were altered to have 1 in. diameter elements and the number was reduced to 36, which was the arrangement as applied to subsequent examples of the '4500' Class. No. 4554 had been further modified from its original condition by having cab shutters added, as well as outside steam pipes. The locomotive was withdrawn from Penzance shed in September 1958. On the 23rd May 1971 St Ives station re-opened after being moved slightly to the east and the view from this position would now feature the station's car park.

Above

St Erth Station 1028

'County' Class 4-6-0 no. 1028 *County of Warwick* has also been caught by Bill departing from the east end of St Erth station with 'The Cornishman' service on 1st September 1960. The station was opened on 11th March 1852 as St Ives Road by the W.C.R. and the name change occurred upon the installation of the St Ives branch; the platform serving the line can be seen hosting a train on the right. After departing from Bath Road depot *County of Warwick* moved only a short distance to Bristol St Phillip's Marsh shed and worked from there until November 1963 when removed to Swindon. The locomotive stayed for a month before being sent for scrap; the engine was the only class member to leave service during December 1963.

Above
Swindon Shed 7029
'Castle' Class engine no. 7029 *Clun Castle* had its picture taken at Swindon shed by Bill, while another photographer takes a more detailed view of the cab from the tender. The shed featured in this image was located on the east side of the line to Gloucester and was a composite of three buildings. The first structure to be completed was a nine-road dead-end shed in 1871 and then in 1892 a roundhouse was affixed to the northern end. The final addition was another roundhouse which adjoined to the eastern wall in 1908. The complex was open until October 1964 and later demolished; the land is now occupied by an industrial estate.

Opposite
Swindon Shed 7022
On the 9th May 1964 Bill was part of the Midland Branch of the Railway Correspondence and Travel Society's 'The East Midlander' railtour which travelled from Nottingham Victoria station to Didcot behind Stanier 'Coronation' Class Pacific no. 46251 *City of Nottingham*. Bulleid 'West Country' Light Pacific no. 34038 *Lynton* then took the train on a jaunt around the Southern Region before dropping the party at Swindon for the return to Nottingham with no. 46251. While at Swindon the passengers were afforded the opportunity of looking at the shed and works, with Bill only too happy to take portraits of the assembled motive power. Visiting from Worcester was 'Castle' Class locomotive no. 7022 *Hereford Castle*. The engine was a recent transfer to the depot, having arrived in April from Hereford. By October no. 7022 had been moved to Gloucester Horton Road and withdrawal would occur there in June 1965.

Below

Swindon Station 7020

'Castle' Class locomotive no. 7020 *Gloucester Castle* was built at Swindon Works in May 1949. As new the engine was fitted with a three-row superheater and Hawksworth straight-sided 4,000 gallon tender. The HC-type boiler, which was used on no. 7020, had 170 small tubes, 21 superheater flues and 84 elements, with the former having a heating surface of 1,799.5 sq. ft and the latter two combined to provide 313 sq. ft. The superheater heating surface was later reduced when the elements were shortened and became 295 sq. ft. *Gloucester Castle* was subsequently fitted with a boiler possessing a four-row superheater (HD-type) in February 1961 and at the same time acquired a double chimney and was re-attached to a Hawksworth tender after carrying a Collett 4,000 gallon tender for a number of years. The four-row superheater increased the heating surface to 380.5 sq. ft, while there was also a reduction in the number of small tubes to 138 and the heating surface became 1,670.10 sq. ft. No. 7020 carried the HD-type boiler until withdrawal in September 1964.

Above
Swindon Station 2879
No. 2879 of the '2800' Class was constructed at Swindon Works as part of lot no. 210 in March 1919. The lot comprised 28 engines and they differentiated themselves from the locomotives constructed previously by having their frame arrangements changed through the addition of metal castings to increase adhesion; no. 2846 was the prototype for this modification. Afterwards the weight of the locomotives was appreciably increased from 68 tons 6 cwt to 75 tons 10 cwt. Other differences included the livery, which was green in place of black with red lining, and the chimney. Two types were fitted to the lot; a large cast-iron chimney was fitted to the first eight, while the remainder had a slight variation on the standard copper capped chimney. No. 2879 had provided the G.W.R. and B.R. with over 45 years' service when it was condemned in August 1964.

Below
Swindon Station 18000

This strange-looking arrival at Swindon station is gas turbine-electric locomotive no. 18000. The G.W.R. instigated the foray into this form of traction (of which there were two other examples running during the 1950s and 1960s for B.R.) in 1946 when it placed an order with Brown, Boveri & Cie of Switzerland. The turbine of no. 18000 drove an electric generator and in turn this powered four traction motors - two for each bogie. A heat exchanger was also employed to recover heat from the exhaust to improve efficiency. The gas turbine technology was attractive to the G.W.R. because it offered double the horsepower of diesel locomotives being produced at the time and this fell more in line with the output of the company's express passenger steam engines. No. 18000 arrived in England during February 1950 and, after working a number of trials, was taken into stock in May 1950. During the next decade in service between London, Plymouth and Bristol the locomotive was found to have a high fuel consumption and difficult to maintain, leading to withdrawal during 1960. After four years being stored at Swindon, the locomotive returned to the continent as a test vehicle and was later displayed in Vienna. In the early 1990s no. 18000 came back to England, minus its gas turbine, and has been exhibited a number of times subsequently.

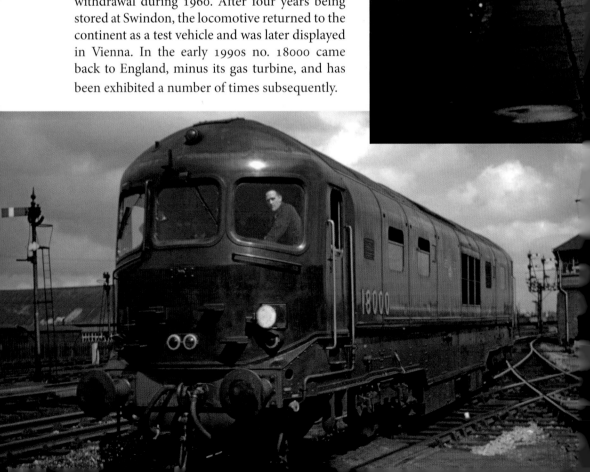

Above

Swindon Station 6010

'King' Class 4-6-0 no. 6010 *King Charles I* awaits the signal to allow departure from platform six at Swindon station. The thirty members of the 'King' Class were constructed to handle the heaviest passenger services and to allow even longer trains to be operated by the G.W.R. For the increased power needed to achieve this aim, the engines required a new boiler working at 250 psi, larger diameter cylinders and coupled wheels 6 ft 6 in. diameter. To accommodate the heavy new class on their system, the company increased the maximum permissible axle loads on the main lines from London to Wolverhampton and Plymouth to 22½ tons. To display that the engine was in compliance with this restriction, but over the previous highest axle load (20 tons) the G.W.R. introduced the 'double red' axle load cab-side discs and these are visible in this picture. No. 6010 was erected in April 1928 and had a service life of 34 years, being withdrawn in June 1962.

Above
Swindon Station 5963

This smart-looking 'Hall' Class locomotive is carrying an '82D' shedcode which signifies that no. 5963 *Wimpole Hall* was based from Westbury depot at the time this image was recorded on film. This allocation lasted from February 1956 to February 1963. Subsequently, St Phillip's Marsh shed housed the engine until it was taken out of traffic in June 1964.

Below
Swindon Station 2838
Swindon station was opened on 31st May 1841 by the G.W.R. and on a few occasions has been referred to as Swindon Junction in the company timetable and *Bradshaw's Guide*. The station has subsequently undergone some alterations. These include the removal of the footbridge over the main lines and the erection of a twelve-storey office block on the southern side of the station that now forms the entrance. Returning to the twilight of the original station's heyday, Churchward '2800' Class 2-8-0 no. 2838 passes through with a freight train. The locomotive was the third member of the class to be built as part of lot no. 186 in September 1912. As built, no. 2838 had a group 97 boiler with 176 small tubes, 14 superheater flues and 84 superheater elements; the boiler also possessed a top feed. The engine had a prolonged residency at Severn Tunnel Junction during the B.R. period and ended its career there in August 1959.

Below

Swindon Works 7029

The G.W.R's first 'Superintendent of Locomotive Engines' Daniel Gooch chose Swindon to be the site of the company's locomotive repair works in 1840 and this was subsequently approved by Isambard Kingdom Brunel and the Board of Directors. Work on the facilities, on land to the north west of the station, was completed in January 1843 and there were two buildings capable of housing 66 engines under repair. The first locomotive to be built at the works was 'Premier' Class 0-6-0 goods engine *Premier* in February 1846, but this had a boiler made by a contractor. The first true Swindon engine was 2-2-2 locomotive *Great Western* which appeared in April 1846. The works reached its zenith in the 1930s when it covered approximately 323 acres. No. 7029 is pictured outside 'A' Shop which covered 11½ acres and contained the wheel shop, boiler shop, erecting shop, machine and fitting shop and repair shop; the majority of the shops contained a number of pits served by an electric traverser.

Above

Swindon Works 6022

'King' Class locomotive no. 6022 *King Edward III* stands out of action at Swindon Works. The engine was completed there in June 1930 as the second of four to be erected during the course of the month. Upon entering traffic, *King Edward III* was allocated to Plymouth Laira and the locomotive was again noted at the depot at Nationalisation. The shed always had a high concentration of the class and reached its height during the mid-1950s when twelve 'Kings' called the depot home. In May 1956 no. 6022 was fitted with a double chimney during a visit to the works and, during the previous year, the engine had undergone a transfer to Old Oak Common. The final residence for *King Edward III* was Wolverhampton Stafford Road and this comprised the period from July 1959 to September 1962.

Above

Talyllyn Junction Station 4679

'8750' Class 0-6-0PT locomotive no. 4679 is seen at Talyllyn Junction station with the 3.00 p.m. Newport to Brecon service on 21st April 1962. The station would only remain open for a short time as closure occurred on 31st December 1962, bringing to an end 93 years of services for the local community. Talyllyn Junction replaced a temporary station known as Talyllyn Brynderwen, which had been opened on 23rd April 1863 by the Brecon & Merthyr Railway on the company's line from the former to Pant. Later, the line was joined with the Pontypridd, Caerphilly & Newport Railway at Bassaleg Junction, allowing access to Newport. The B.&M.R. was also later connected to the Mid-Wales Railway with the opening of the company's line from Llanidloes in 1864. Both the M.W.R. and B.&M.R. lines were closed at the time of the station. No. 4679 survived until May 1965.

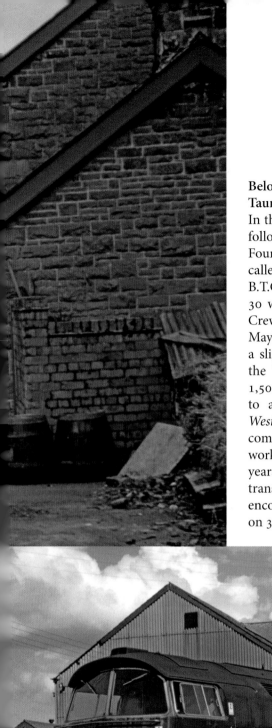

Below

Taunton Shed D1072

In the wake of the design for the 'Warship' Class followed plans for an even more powerful Type Four diesel-hydraulic locomotive, later to be called the 'Western' Class, and in mid-1959 the B.T.C. allowed 74 to be ordered. In the event, 30 were constructed by Swindon Works, while Crewe Works provided the remaining 44. The Maybach 12-cylinder MD 655 engines used were a slightly modified version of that employed in the 'Warship' Class and produced 1,350 hp at 1,500 rpm. A change in transmission was made to a Voith L630rV three-speed unit. D1072 *Western Glory* was the penultimate engine to be completed at Crewe in November 1963 and it worked from Old Oak Common for the first few years of its time in service. The locomotive had transferred to Plymouth Laira by the time Bill encountered it between duties at Taunton shed on 3rd August 1967.

Below
Tavistock South Station 5572
This image of '4575' Class 2-6-2T no. 5572 was taken at Tavistock South station on 11th August 1961. No. 5572 was amongst the final five class members to enter traffic during February 1929 and one of two of these to begin work at Exeter St David's shed. By 1961 the engine had undertaken a number of moves and was residing at Plymouth Laira, which was destined to be its last depot, and withdrawal occurred in April 1962. Tavistock South station, opened on 22nd June 1859 as Tavistock by the South Devon & Tavistock Railway, would also be taken out of use during 1962, closure coming on 31st December.

Above
Tiverton Junction Station 1440
A freight service from Tiverton station arrives at Tiverton Junction station behind '1400' Class 0-4-2T locomotive no. 1440. The station was opened by the Bristol & Exeter Railway on 1st May 1844 as Tiverton Road, but renaming occurred on 12th December 1848, six months after the opening of the four-mile branch to Tiverton. No. 1440 was built at Swindon in March 1935, renumbered in October 1946 and condemned in December 1963.

Below

Tiverton Junction Station 1434

Another '1400' Class member present at Tiverton Junction station was no. 1434 and the engine is in charge of a mixed service to Hemyock. The latter place was the terminus of the Culm Valley Light Railway which opened on 29th May 1876 from Tiverton Junction and the route was worked by the G.W.R. until the company absorbed the former in 1880. The line closed to passengers on 9th September 1963, but remained open to freight and a local dairy until 1965 and 1975 respectively. Tiverton Junction station was also subsequently closed and replaced by Tiverton Parkway which opened on 12th May 1986. No. 1434 was constructed at Swindon in July 1934 and withdrawn from Exeter St David's depot during July 1962.

Above

Truro Station 1007

Hawksworth 'County' Class locomotive no. 1007 *County of Brecknock* has the signal which allows it to depart from Truro station. The engine entered traffic in December 1945 and was bestowed with the name of the county in Wales during January 1948. Thus, no. 1007 was one of the class members nameless in service for the longest period; no. 1006 was unnamed for a further four months of its career. *County of Brecknock* was allocated to Bristol Bath Road depot during the early portion of its career, but by early 1955 had been transferred to Truro, spending over four years there. The 'County' Class had a red weight restriction limiting the locomotives to routes where an axle load of 20 tons was permissible. The Class' 'D' power classification is also seen in no. 1007's weight restriction disc. *County of Brecknock* moved to Exeter and Didcot before being condemned in October 1962.

Below

Wadebridge Station 4666

Wadebridge was one of the first places to boast a railway as the Bodmin & Wadebridge Railway opened their system on 1st October 1834. However, the local population used the services sparingly and the line was mainly used for freight traffic. The London & South Western Railway subsequently bought the line in 1847 as a strategic move against the G.W.R. and other competitors, but relations between the two later became amicable and the G.W.R. connected to the line in 1888 at Boscarne Junction. Prior to this the L.&S.W.R. closed the B.&W.R. route for major reconstruction work and upon reopening a new station at Wadebridge was inaugurated on 3rd September 1888. '8750' Class 0-6-0PT no. 4666 is pictured at the station on 1st September 1960. Seven years later the station would be closed, but it survives today at the John Betjeman Centre.

Above
Truro Station 6873
'Grange' Class 4-6-0 no. 6873 *Caradoc Grange* takes an empty wagon train out of the west end of Truro station during the early 1960s. The public footbridge is in the background, in addition to the goods yard, while on the left Truro West signal box is visible. The latter two features have since been removed, but Truro East signal box is still in use.

Above

Westbury 4924

During April 1958, immaculate 'Hall' Class locomotive no. 4924 *Eydon Hall* posed for Bill's camera at Westbury station. The engine entered traffic from Swindon in May 1929 and performed its duties until October 1963 when condemned to be scrapped. *Eydon Hall* has been pictured while Banbury-allocated and this lasted for the period between November 1957 to July 1959. The locomotive's last residency was at Swindon, where no. 4924 spent eleven months. Westbury station was opened by the Wiltshire, Somerset & Weymouth Railway on 5th September 1848 as the final station on the line from Thingley Junction, near Chippenham, which was on the G.W.R. line from London to Bristol. However, the W.S.&W.R. soon handed over control of the route, and the obligation to construct the remainder, to the G.W.R.

Below

Wellington Salop Station 6007

Two locomotives present at Wellington station, situated on the line between Birmingham and Shrewsbury, on 12th June 1962, were 'King' Class 4-6-0 no. 6007 *King William III* and Ivatt Class 2 2-6-2T no. 41232. The latter was constructed at Crewe Works in August 1949 and, after spells at Chester and Wrexham, transferred to Wellington shed in February 1960, being employed by the depot until February 1964. *King William III* was employed by Wolverhampton Stafford Road shed when this picture was taken and had arrived there from Plymouth Laira in October 1959. No. 6007 would soon leave traffic, but no. 41232 continued to work until August 1965 when withdrawal from Llandudno Junction occurred. Wellington station had the Salop portion of its title added in 1951 to avoid confusion with the station of the same name in Somerset. But it was later removed to allow 'Telford' to be inserted to denote the proximity of the new town before being removed when Telford Central was opened on the Wolverhampton-Shrewsbury line.

Below

Wellington Station 6155

'6100' Class 2-6-2T no. 6155 is pictured at Somerset's Wellington station. The station was located close to Taunton on the line from the town to Exeter and was opened by the Bristol & Exeter Railway on 1st May 1843. The station had 'Som' added to its name in 1951, but was subsequently closed on 5th October 1964 as a result of the Beeching Report. No. 6155 was erected at Swindon Works in March 1933, being the second of six class members to enter traffic during this month. The locomotive's first allocation was to Slough and at Nationalisation it was to Old Oak Common. The locomotive had a spell at Severn Tunnel Junction in the late 1950s before being transferred to Taunton and the engine was probably working from the depot at the time of this photograph. No. 6155's last allocation was to Worcester and the engine was condemned at the shed in October 1965.

Above

Wellington Salop Station 9639

Wellington served as the centre for a number of railway construction projects between the 1840s and 1860s. The first saw the Shrewsbury & Birmingham Railway and the Shropshire Union Railways & Canal Co. join forces to link Wolverhampton with Shrewsbury. The former company opened their first section between Wellington and Oakengates on 1st June 1849, while the latter company constructed the section from Shrewsbury to Wellington and a line from Stafford to Wellington, both sections being opened on the same day as the above. The S.&B.R. was taken over by the G.W.R. in the mid-1850s, and the latter also took over the Wellington and Severn Junction Railway in the early 1860s. During this decade the G.W.R. also formed a connection from Wellington to Market Drayton and the already built Nantwich & Market Drayton Railway, therefore providing the G.W.R. with their own route to Crewe. '8750' Class 0-6-0PT locomotive no. 9639 stands at Wellington station with a branch passenger service on 12th June 1962.

Below
Westbury Shed 6358
Westbury Shed was the location for this picture of '4300' Class 2-6-0 no. 6358 and it was taken during April 1958. The locomotive had resided at the shed since mid-1953 and would remain there until withdrawal in October 1959. No. 6358 is in B.R. unlined black livery, but some members of the class had lined green livery applied towards the end of the 1950s and several engines were also painted in unlined green. Westbury shed was located to the west of the station and on the south side of the line. The four-track depot was opened by the G.W.R. in February 1915 and was in use until September 1965.

Above

Whitchurch Station 5322

'4300' Class 2-6-0 no. 5322 waits to depart from platform four with the 2.05 p.m. service from Whitchurch station to Welshpool on 11th June 1962. Constructed in August 1917 at Swindon Works, no. 5322 saw active service in the First World War along with ten other class members, which were used to haul munitions and hospital trains. After the cessation of hostilities no. 5322 entered traffic for the G.W.R. in 1919 and was then in service for the company and B.R. until April 1964 when it was sent to be scrapped at Woodham Brothers, Barry. However, in the late 1960s the locomotive was bought for restoration and after a period of inactivity returned to service at the Didcot Railway Centre. Whitchurch station was opened by the London & North Western Railway on 1st September 1858 as part of the Crewe & Shrewsbury Railway.

Below

Worcester Shed W24W

The G.W.R. made its first foray into using internal combustion engines for traffic purposes in 1911 when the company ordered a railcar powered by a petrol engine. However, this was relatively unsuccessful and it was 1933 before a second railcar, powered by a diesel engine, entered service. Evidently this application was a triumph as 38, albeit with a number of modifications, were subsequently constructed between 1934 and 1942. W24W emerged from Swindon Works in September 1940 and featured two 121 horsepower Associated Equipment Co. Ltd diesel engines, seating for 48 and standard drawgear. Pictured at Worcester shed on 7th April 1962, the railcar would be condemned by October.

Above

Whitland Station 5550

'4575' Class 2-6-2T no. 5550 was seen by Bill at Whitland station with the 10.45 a.m. service to Pembroke Dock on 21st April 1962. The locomotive was constructed at Swindon Works in October 1928 and its first allocation was to Ebbw Junction, where it was again noted at Nationalisation. But, in November 1952 no. 5550 made the move to Neyland, which had Whitland amongst its sub-sheds, and remained there until withdrawal in September 1962. Whitland station was opened by the South Wales Railway on 2nd January 1854, being part of the line built to Haverfordwest; when completed the line stretched from Gloucester to Neyland. The Pembroke & Tenby Railway installed the branch line to Pembroke Dock and this was operational from 8th August 1864, running from a station opposite the S.W.R's building because of differing gauges. The latter company's facilities became the host for both lines from August 1869.

Below

Worcester Shed 7021

The locomotive shed at Worcester was located to the north of Shrub Hill station on land between the line to Hereford and Kidderminster. The depot was a four-track through road building and, later, a three-road shed was added close by, but the installation dates for both structures is unknown. 'Castle' Class 4-6-0 no. 7021 *Haverfordwest Castle* was erected at Swindon in June 1949 and went to work from Landore. In time, no. 7021 would spend much of its career in south Wales with allocations to Carmarthen and Llanelly. *Haverfordwest Castle* was fitted with a double chimney in November 1961, in addition to a type-HD boiler, providing some indication to the date of the image. The locomotive also has an '81A' shed code revealing that Old Oak Common shed maintained the engine at this time; no. 7021 would be removed from service from the depot in September 1963. Worcester shed closed to steam traffic in December 1965 and subsequently spent 20 years servicing diesel locomotives.

Above

Worcester Foregate Street Station W33W

G.W.R. twin railcar, consisting of W33W and W38W, has arrived at Worcester Foregate Street station, which was the first stop for this branch service destined for Bromyard after starting from Worcester Shrub Hill station. Foregate Street station was opened by the Worcester & Hereford Railway on 17th May 1860 on the second section of the company's line to be completed. The Worcester, Bromyard & Leominster Railway installed the branch line. The company was beset by financial problems and, after receiving permission for the line in 1861, did not open the first section between Leominster Junction, on the W.&H.R. line, and Bromyard until 22nd October 1877. The section to Leominster was only finished after the G.W.R. purchased the W.,B.&L.R. once it had been liquidated and the full extent of the line was ready for traffic on 1st September 1897. This twin railcar originally comprised W37W and W38W, but the former was damaged by a fire and later condemned, necessitating the conversion of W33W to fit in the set. The image dates from 7th April 1962 and the twin railcar would be withdrawn in August. The line between Bromyard and Leominster was closed on 15th September 1952, while the Worcester to Bromyard section survived until 7th September 1964.

Worcester Shrub Hill Station 5056
The Oxford, Worcester & Wolverhampton Railway and Midland Railway jointly opened Worcester Shrub Hill station on 5th October 1850. Leaving the station for the Capital on 16th April 1963 was 'Castle' Class locomotive no. 5056 *Earl of Powis* with the 15.10 service. The locomotive was built at Swindon Works in June 1936, originally

being named *Ogmore Castle*, but the change transpired a short time later in September 1937. A long-term Old Oak Common resident, *Earl of Powis* was only three months away from a move to Cardiff East Dock, then in 1964, the engine had brief spells at Hereford and Oxley before withdrawal occurred in November. Eight 'Castle' class engines have been preserved.

Bibliography

Christiansen, R. *Rail Centres: Crewe.* 2007.

Clark, R.H. *An Historical Survey of Selected Great Western Stations; Layouts and Illustrations.* 1976.

Clough, David N. *British Rail Standard Diesels of the 1960s.* 2009.

Dow, George. *Great Central: Volume Three Fay Sets the Pace, 1900-1922.* 1985.

Griffiths, Roger and Paul Smith. *The Directory of British Engine Sheds and Principal Locomotive Servicing Points: 1 Southern England, the Midlands, East Anglia and Wales.* 1999.

Quick, Michael. *Railway Passenger Stations in Great Britain: A Chronology.* 2009.

R.C.T.S. *The Locomotives of the Great Western Railway: Part Two Broad Gauge.* 1952.

R.C.T.S. *The Locomotives of the Great Western Railway: Part Three Absorbed Engines 1854-1921.* 1956.

R.C.T.S. *The Locomotives of the Great Western Railway: Part Four Six-Wheeled Tender Engines.* 1956.

R.C.T.S. *The Locomotives of the Great Western Railway: Part Five Six-Coupled Tank Engines.* 1958.

R.C.T.S. *The Locomotives of the Great Western Railway: Part Six Four-Coupled Tank Engines.* 1959.

R.C.T.S. *The Locomotives of the Great Western Railway: Part Seven Dean's Larger Tender Engines.* 1954.

R.C.T.S. *The Locomotives of the Great Western Railway: Part Eight Modern Passenger Classes.* 1960.

R.C.T.S. *The Locomotives of the Great Western Railway: Part Nine Standard Two-Cylinder Classes.* 1962.

R.C.T.S. *The Locomotives of the Great Western Railway: Part Ten Absorbed Engines 1922-1947.* 1966.

R.C.T.S. *The Locomotives of the Great Western Railway: Part Eleven The Rail Motor Vehicles and Internal Combustion Locomotives.* 1956.

R.C.T.S. *The Locomotives of the Great Western Railway: Part Twelve A Chronological and Statistical Survey.* 1974.

R.C.T.S. *A Detailed History of British Railways Standard Steam Locomotives Volume Four: The 9F 2-10-0 Class.* 2008.

Vernon, Tony. *Yorkshire Engine Company: Sheffield's Locomotive Manufacturer.* 2008.